D1541527

I'M ALL RIGHT

A JOURNEY FROM TRAGEDY TO TRIUMPH

Jer. 17:5-8

"Living in the moment and trusting God through the good times and the bad is a key for every individual who is a follower of Jesus. The way Bryan has dealt with the highs and lows of life is an encouragement and inspiration to anyone who has experienced the reality of facing tragedy and victory. That Sunday evening in June changed everything for him, except his faith in Christ and trust in God's abiding presence. You will rejoice in God's goodness as you read Bryan's story because he has walked in triumph in the midst of his grief and loss."

Stephen R. Tourville, D. Min.
PennDel Ministry Network
Superintendent

"The night of the accident, Bryan's mother said to me, 'Bryan is going to have a powerful testimony when he gets through this.' She was so right! This book is that story.

"It is epic and will deeply impact you and draw you closer to God, as you learn how Bryan navigated game-changing moments and trusted a God who turned tragedy into hope. You will especially want to share this book with the men of your church!"

Tom Rees
PennDel Ministry Network
Church Planting and Development
Men's Ministry Director

"Bryan Koch is one of my heroes. His story, *I'm All Right*, tells about the fateful day of June 7, 2015, when he and his wife, Lynn, while on a motorcycle ride were struck by a drunk driver. Lynn was killed instantly and Bryan barely clung to life for weeks. Four months later Bryan was back in the pulpit as pastor of one of the largest churches in the Assemblies of God. I've seen firsthand the impact of his life and testimony on the community of Reading, Pennsylvania, and beyond. You will see in his story the great truth he articulated to me when I had the privilege of ministering to his congregation in April, 2016: 'If God brought you to it, He will bring you through it.' This book imparts hope to anyone going through trial – The Lord will indeed bring YOU through it."

George O. Wood
General Superintendent
Assemblies of God

I'M ALL RIGHT

A JOURNEY FROM TRAGEDY TO TRIUMPH

B R Y A N   K O C H

with **B E T S Y   F I C K**

Endless
Press

Dedicated to my boys, their wives, and my grandchildren, in memory of Lynn.

Endless Press
15 S Church St
Spring City, PA 19475
Info@EndlessPress.org
www.EndlessPress.org

ISBN 978-0-9862250-9-3

BISAC: BIO018000 BIOGRAPHY & AUTOBIOGRAPHY / Religious

Contents

Chapter 1

Left Thinking

June 7, 2015

How do you know what your life will be like tomorrow?
Your life is like the morning fog—it's here a little while,
then it's gone.
James 4:14 (NLT)

June 7 started like any other ordinary Sunday. Bryan and Lynn Koch woke up and went about their normal Sunday morning routine before heading to GT Church, where Bryan was the lead pastor of a congregation of close to three thousand, and Lynn had become an ordained pastor just weeks earlier. The church was kicking off a new sermon series about biblical friendship that weekend, and that morning's service was planned around honoring the community's first responders. Special guests had been invited and the GT team was ready for an exciting morning.

When they arrived at GT, the church was just starting to buzz with the morning's activities. Fire trucks were parked out front with ladders raised in a tribute to the dedicated men and women who put their lives on the line to save others. Kids, fresh out of school for the summer, were sporting matching blue t-shirts as excitement started to build for the church's upcoming Vacation Bible School. The smell of summer was in the air, and the church campus was alive as hundreds of attendees and volunteers began arriving on that beautiful Sunday morning.

Church went exactly as planned with a powerful service in which Bryan recognized first responders from both the church and community. He then preached a message about being the kind of person who runs toward danger and disaster in an effort to lend a helping hand instead of running away from it. His sermon that day inspired many in the church congregation to put others first, both in prayer and in their daily lives, just as first responders are called to do day in and day out. And as he preached on the parable of the Good Samaritan, he challenged the church to be a friend to others when no one else will.

That Sunday morning was counted as a success. It was a big day for the community, a big day for GT, and a great kick off to the summer series. Bryan and Lynn left church and looked forward to enjoying the beautiful afternoon ahead. As they often did after church, they went out for lunch with some family and friends and chatted about the day and life over burgers and milkshakes.

The couple arrived home after a busy morning and early afternoon, and were relaxing when Lynn suggested that they go out for a motorcycle ride to take advantage of the weather. Bryan and Lynn were both avid motorcyclists and frequently took rides together, with Lynn often being the one to initiate the plans. Many times Bryan would come home and Lynn would have mowed the grass and taken care of other things around the house so that nothing would stand in the way of them being able to get out on the road and spend some time together on their bike.

Not wanting to waste a gorgeous afternoon, the pair got dressed for their ride, prayed together for safety (as they always did), and hit the road, headed toward one of Lynn's favorite spots, The Pretzel Hut, in Lancaster, Pennsylvania. The drive to Lancaster was beautiful. The sun sparkled over the farm fields, lush with crops and rows of corn just starting to peek their green heads through the soil. The sky seemed cloudless and the drive was an easy one.

When they arrived at The Pretzel Hut, they sat in the sun, eating ice cream and chatting about the big changes they had coming up in their lives. After twenty-eight years of marriage, Bryan and Lynn were getting ready to become grandparents as their oldest son, Ben, and his wife, Jen, would be welcoming a son into their family later that year. Their middle son, Bryce, had just graduated with his bachelor's degree and had accepted a job in Ohio, and their youngest, Brett, would be heading into his senior year of high school in the fall.

It was an exciting season for the couple. A season full of change, but one of hope, expectation, and anticipation as they prepared to have an empty nest at home, and then to fill that home with the laughter of grandchildren.

They finished their ice cream and got on the bike as they headed back toward home, enjoying the rest of their ride. Everything seemed perfect on that Sunday: the weather, the time spent together, even the couple as they looked forward to the next chapter in their lives.

A mile from their house, they made the familiar turn onto Grange Road. It was a road they had traveled many times as they came to and from their home. Bryan knew it was a dangerous stretch filled with sharp turns that people often took faster than they should, and so as a measure of precaution, he always stayed toward the outside of his lane. There were no signs of danger, however, on that particular day. Everything seemed calm and normal as Bryan and Lynn's ride was coming to an end and they began thinking about the week ahead.

Moments later, an SUV crossed the center line while careening around a bend and collided with Bryan and Lynn's motorcycle. And in a matter of seconds on June 7, everything changed.

A recent portrait of Bryan and Lynn Koch.
Photo courtesy of Dave Zerbe Studio/Bonita Zerbe.

June 7, 2015 – At the scene of the accident, Bryan's Harley was pinned under an SUV. Photo courtesy of Greenfields Fire Company/Steve Spies

Chapter 2

Left Crushed

Ronda & Renee – June 7, 2015

*If you openly declare that Jesus is Lord and believe in
your heart that God raised him from the dead, you will
be saved. For it is by believing in your heart that you
are made right with God, and it is by openly declaring
your faith that you are saved.*
Romans 10:9-10 (NLT)

Ronda Neiswender was on her way home from GT
Church on Sunday, June 7, when an odd sensation
came over her. On the short, fifteen-minute drive
she suddenly felt an overwhelming sadness and a
feeling of fear swept through her mind. In the middle
of a gorgeous summer day, it felt like the world was
suddenly dark and void of hope.

She did a quick mental checklist of her family,
running through her husband, Dave, and their two
children, her sisters, Lynn and Renee, and their

families, and everyone was accounted for as safe. But for a few minutes, Ronda felt as if she was in a freefall. As quickly as the feeling came, it was gone, and Ronda finished her drive, but she couldn't quite shake how strange the experience was.

That afternoon, Renee came over to pick up her children who had been playing with their cousins. The kids had all just finished their school year and were looking forward to the summer. As the two sisters sat out on Ronda's back porch chatting about their summer plans and talking about vacations, Dave came to the door and handed Ronda the phone. It was Bryce.

"Aunt Ronda, I just got out of the shower and there's a message here from the Reading Hospital and they have Dad there. They said there was an accident."

Confused, Ronda asked, "Bryce, why didn't Lynn call you?"

"I don't know," replied Bryce. "They said they don't know where she is."

That was all Ronda needed to hear. She and Renee immediately hopped in the car to meet Bryce at the hospital, all the while checking their phones, expecting Lynn to call at any moment. As they drove they began to pray and were fighting off every possibility, including the worst. When Ronda finally managed to mutter the thought aloud, "Renee...what if..." the two sisters dismissed it as soon as it came. It was probably just a few broken bones, and they could all handle that together.

The sisters arrived at the Reading Hospital's emergency room, where they went through the hospital's rudimentary security procedures. The simple process of checking in felt like it took forever to Ronda and Renee, and when they finally got into the hospital, they were sent from the triage desk to the security guard, where Renee spotted a piece of paper. The paper simply read: Bryan Koch...taken to the OR.

Immediately Ronda thought, "Ok, we have Bryan's paper, where's Lynn's paper?"

At that moment Bryce walked through the door and joined Ronda and Renee at the desk. They began firing questions at the security guard: "Where's Lynn? Where's our sister? Where's his mother? Was she taken upstairs already?"

The security guard simply replied, "You need to wait here for the chaplain."

The notion seemed comical to Ronda, Renee, and Bryce. "A chaplain? Why on earth would we need a chaplain? Bryan is a pastor! We have oodles of them over at the church! We don't need a chaplain!" But quietly they waited, while inside, their frustrations, emotions, and anxieties were beginning to escalate. Eventually, a sweet woman met them and introduced herself as the hospital's chaplain.

As the chaplain led them down a hallway, frustration began to take over. And the questions came again. "Where's Lynn? Where's our sister? Where's his mother?"

"We don't know. We don't know," was the only reply anyone could seem to offer them.

Moment by moment they were getting more and more distraught. They were taken to a small private waiting room, still with no answer concerning Lynn's whereabouts. It was like Lynn had just disappeared into thin air. They began calling other hospitals, wondering whether Lynn was even with Bryan on the bike. Was she in the OR? Was she upstairs waiting for Bryan to come out of surgery? They tried to consider every possible scenario but kept coming up with nothing.

Then there was a knock on the door and a trauma surgeon entered the room. He still had his mask on, fresh out of surgery, and he began to give the sisters and their nephew a detailed account of Bryan's injuries. "He's lost a lot of blood...he had to be resuscitated at the scene and then one more time here at the hospital...his leg...amputated above the knee..."

In that moment, time stood still. The sisters couldn't hear anything else that the surgeon said after that. All Ronda could think was, "Amputated... but Bryan used to be a catcher. Bryan's a big guy... he used to swing his nieces and nephews around in the swimming pool...how do we tell him that his leg is gone?"

Sitting next to her, Renee's head was spinning. "This is really bad...this is more than just a few broken bones. It's bad."

"...and his liver was lacerated. We had to remove his spleen and there's a bleed on the brain but we're not overly concerned about that right now."

Renee looked over at Bryce and thought "He's only twenty-two years old. He just graduated from college, he's about to begin his life." Bryce just sat there, suddenly looking small to his aunt as he just kept nodding at the doctor and muttering "ok" over and over. She wished she could just pick him up in her arms and make the bad news go away. But she couldn't.

"We're supposed to be the adults," she thought. "We have to be the ones to hold it together."

As Ronda and Renee tried to be strong for their nephew, they felt panic beginning to rise inside.

And then they asked again, "But where's Lynn? Where's our sister? Where's his mother?" and yet again, they were met with nothing. The doctor only had news about Bryan.

The surgeon left them alone to try to process the news of Bryan's condition, but the question of "Where's Lynn?" echoed in the room like a distant scream. The chaplain, still sitting with the three of them, began making a few phone calls. She paused her calls to ask them questions: "What was she wearing? What name did Lynn go by?" The three of them quickly answered as many of her questions as they could, but her inquiries only sparked more uncertainty for Ronda and Renee.

Trying to speed the process along, Renee called her husband, John, to see if he had heard any news. After what seemed like hours, the chaplain hung up the phone for the last time. "There's an unidentified, deceased female at the scene." Her eyes were pained with sadness as she muttered the words Ronda and Renee would never forget.

In that moment, their world changed forever... Lynn was dead. They knew that if Bryan's injuries were that bad, there was no way Lynn could have survived. She had to be the "unidentified female." It felt like the air had been sucked out of the tiny room.

The sisters couldn't breathe; they didn't know what to do and felt like they were in a freefall.

Shaking, Renee typed out three words to John through a text message, "Send the pastors."

Ronda picked up the phone, called her husband Dave, and simply muttered, "You've gotta get here, it's not looking good."

With heads down as if walking in slow motion, they followed the chaplain upstairs to a conference room off of a larger waiting area and all they could think about was how this was going to change so many lives.

And then people started to arrive. Family, pastors, and friends all began to gather in the ICU's waiting room. At one point Ronda and Renee went down the hall, and when they turned the corner into the waiting area they saw it was filled with friends and staff from GT. The sisters just stood there, amazed at how many people were there to support their family and Bryan. Dozens of people just sat there, looking at them, everyone unsure of the details of what was happening and what anyone could say or do to make it all better.

After a few hours of waiting in the conference room with the rest of the family, the coroner finally arrived at 11:00 pm with camera in hand. He entered the room and spoke briefly with the family; he needed someone to identify Lynn's body. Bryan's dad, Ted, volunteered and after peering at a small screen on the back of the camera, uttered the words, "It's her."

Then Dave and John followed, "It's her, it's her."

Inside, Ronda and Renee were screaming, "No! It's not her! It can't be. We just saw her and heard her voice a few hours ago at church!"

The coroner left, and the room fell silent. Ronda and Renee felt sick. Their older sister was dead. Their brother-in-law was fighting for his life and had lost a leg. And their three nephews, at least for the time being, had to face all of this without either parent to help them process the nightmare that they had been thrown into. Ronda's mind hadn't stopped racing all night, but now it was moving from wondering where her sister was to what might happen to Bryan. "What are we going to do if these boys lose both of their parents in one accident? Is he just holding on until his sister gets here?"

John made the phone call to Ronda and Renee's parents to confirm the news they had been dreading, and began helping to coordinate how to get them from where they lived in Ohio to where their daughters were in Pennsylvania.

Not long after the coroner left, a nurse arrived in the family waiting room and began bringing them in small groups to see Bryan, who was now out of surgery and in a room in the hospital's intensive care unit. The sisters stood, looking at Bryan through the hospital room windows, tracing the wires coming out of his body, listening to the beeping of the machines monitoring his every breath. They shook at what they saw, still in disbelief that any of it was real. Bryan, always so full of life, lying there motionless, on life support, missing a leg, not yet knowing that his wife was gone. This couldn't be happening to their family. They entered the room and as Renee approached Bryan's side, she was overwhelmed with a sense of grief greater than anything she had ever experienced. Ronda touched Bryan's arm. "He feels so warm; he feels so alive," she thought to herself. What a contrast to how she felt, as if death and darkness were consuming her.

And then, from behind her, she heard Bryan's mom, Donna, whisper, "Ronda, I pray that you never have to see your son in this condition."

June 7, 2015, split time in half for the two sisters. Before it: life with Lynn; after: life without Lynn. The three girls didn't just share the same DNA or the same maiden name, they shared their lives. They were the best of friends, and their trio had been broken that day.

Chapter 3

Left In Charge

Ben & Jen – June 7, 2015

*The rain came down, the streams rose, and the winds
blew and beat against that house; yet it did not fall,
because it had its foundation on the rock.*
Matthew 7:25 (NIV)

Ben and Jen Koch were on the highway just a few
hours away from the Outer Banks, where they were
spending the week with friends and looking forward
to a relaxing time away at the beach. As they crossed
the border into North Carolina, Jen's cell phone rang.

It was Bryce. He asked to speak to Ben and in an
instant, Jen knew something was wrong. She handed
the phone to Ben and listened as he talked to his
brother. His face grew more concerned the longer
the conversation went on.

"Our dad? Are you sure? Ok, well call them back
and let me know what they say." Ben hung up the

phone and looked over at Jen. The atmosphere in the car suddenly felt thick. "The hospital called the house and left a message," Ben said. "They were looking for Dad's closest kin...they say that Dad's at the hospital. But they probably have the wrong person, right?"

"Right," Jen agreed. "It's probably just a mistake."

The two rode in silence for a little while, trying to keep their worry at bay, until the phone pierced the silence. Once again, it was Bryce, and this time he was distraught. "The hospital said that dad was in an accident and he's in emergency surgery. They don't know where mom is, but they have dad. They're trying to save his life," Bryce said, panicked.

Ben couldn't believe what he was hearing. "Bryce, are you sure? It's definitely our dad? Where's Mom?"

Bryce told Ben that both of their parents had gone on a motorcycle ride that evening. He didn't know where their mom was, but he was going to head to the hospital. Ben told him to call their Aunt Ronda and have her meet him at the hospital as well. He hung up the phone for the second time, this time with even more questions. Where was his mom? Why couldn't anyone get in touch with her? Did the first responders even know she was on the motorcycle with their dad?

Jen and Ben quickly ran through a number of possible explanations for the confusion, all while still heading towards their destination at the beach. Maybe Bryce was wrong? Maybe Lynn hadn't been with Bryan. Or if she was, maybe they took her to a different hospital. It hadn't even occurred to the two that the worst thing they could imagine might be their new reality.

Taking matters into their own hands, Jen called the other hospital in Reading, but they didn't know anything about Lynn either. Ben got on the phone with the Bern Township Police, who had responded to the accident, while Jen called Bryan's sister, Marsha to let her know something serious had happened. The police officer that answered Ben's call didn't offer them much. He just kept telling Ben that they needed to go to the hospital. And finally, Ben uttered the thought that they had both been too scared to speak aloud, "Are they dead?"

On the other end of the line, the police officer just started to cry, "You need to get to the hospital as soon as possible."

Ben hung up the phone and couldn't shake the feeling that both of his parents must be dead for the police officer to have had such an emotional reaction. He immediately called Bryce, who had already made it to the hospital and was able to calm some of Ben's fears when he let him know that Bryan was in emergency surgery. "Ok, well at least that means that he's alive," Ben thought.

Ben called Marsha to give her an update. And then, Jen called Ben's youngest brother, Brett, who was on the way home from some evening events at church. As they were talking, Brett came to Grange Road.

"Hang on, Jen, the road is closed," Brett said as he began to navigate his way around. Before hanging up with him, Jen let him know that his grandparents were waiting for him to get home.

Still unsure of what was really going on back in Pennsylvania, Ben and Jen continued toward North Carolina. Jen called her mom and just asked her parents to start praying. After hanging up the phone with them, Jen's dad started getting in touch with Ben's uncles, and then he called Jen back.

"Honey, there was a female body pronounced dead at the scene of the accident," he said, welling up with emotion.

Ben pulled off the highway and into a parking lot just off the exit. "Ok, what does that mean? What do you think we should do?" Jen asked.

"You need to turn around. We don't know for sure that it's her, but you guys need to come home."

The next call they had to make was to their friends who were expecting them to arrive in the Outer Banks in just a few short hours. As they turned around and started retracing their route back home, they tried to stay positive. They had at least a five-hour drive until they were back in Pennsylvania and could face what was waiting for them at the hospital.

Ben and Jen's drive that night was surreal. It was almost like they were in a bubble. For most of the ride, they had a hard time imagining what was waiting for them at the end of their drive, and so they tried to keep things as normal and light as possible. Each of them knew that the moment they stepped out of the car and through the hospital doors, life as they knew it would change forever.

Around eleven o'clock, Ben's phone rang. It was his grandfather, Ted, calling to confirm their worst fears. He had helped to identify Lynn's body for the coroner at the hospital. The couple was still four hours away from the hospital and they both so badly wanted to just stay in the shelter of the car forever and pretend none of it was happening.

They pulled into the hospital parking lot at three o'clock in the morning. They checked in with the security guard at the front desk, who gave them visitor badges, and made their way upstairs to the intensive care unit. The elevator doors opened to a room full of people: pastors, friends, family members. All eyes were on Ben and Jen and they didn't want to meet any of the stares. The air was heavy with the weight of the evening's events.

They headed into a smaller, private waiting room where the immediate family members were gathered. Ben and Jen collapsed into the familiar hugs of their family, exhausted from driving all day yet wide awake from adrenaline. There were no words to describe what they all were feeling, no real conversations to be had. It wouldn't be long before Ben would be making the medical decisions for his dad as his next-of-kin. In a second, he had to grow up faster than any young adult should ever have to. And overnight, he would be left in charge of making life-changing decisions for his dad.

Shortly after their arrival at the hospital, Ben and Jen crossed through the locked doors into the quiet halls of the intensive care unit, and found their way towards the room where Bryan was lying unconscious in a hospital bed. As they stood there next to his bed, they both silently wondered if this was the last time they'd see him alive.

Chapter 4

Left Hanging in the Balance

June 8, 2015

The Lord is close to the brokenhearted; He rescues those
whose spirits are crushed.
Psalm 34:18 (NLT)

Prayer Request.

The subject line of the email popped up on the phones of GT Church staff across Berks County. These emails weren't unusual for them, but the content of this particular correspondence was unlike anything any of the staff had ever received.

Pastor Bryan and Lynn were in a serious motorcycle accident. Please pray.

That's all it said. No more, no less. And immediately, the phones started to ring as the staff of nearly fifty people tried to figure out what was happening and what they should do. How serious was it? Was the rest of the family ok? When, how, and where did it happen?

It didn't take long before staff members were descending on the hospital and the church, gathering to find answers and comfort in one another's presence, and knowing that as soon as the news broke in the community, people would start to come.

Those who gathered at the hospital filled the waiting room outside of the intensive care unit, quietly exchanging glances, huddled in small groups to cry and pray together, and hanging on any word from the occasional family member who would emerge from the private waiting room down the hall.

Others walked into a dark, quiet church, and at the start the scene was much of the same. But it didn't take long until the news started to spread and people started to show up. The atmosphere in the church's atrium was an odd dichotomy of solemn and busy.

GT's communications team set up camp in one of the atrium seating areas and entered crisis mode, managing the church's social media channels, trying to stop rumors from flying and fiercely protecting the privacy of the family as much as they could, all while trying to process their own emotions. It was the middle of the night, but it felt like the whole world was awake.

At the same time, inside the worship center, the mood was a mix of despair and hope as soft worship music played and people gathered in groups, whispering fervent prayers and shedding countless tears. Each new person who walked into GT's atrium had the same nervous, distraught, and unsure expression and was met with the hug of a staff member or volunteer.

And then, around two o'clock in the morning, the staff at the church sat down to draft the hardest email they'd ever write. They knew that this news would rock their church community. Many of its members would wake up to these words. Which words do you choose to take the sting out of the worst news? What words make the reality less real or less painful? As they drafted, tears drifted down their cheeks and fell in wet splashes on the keyboard.

Last evening, Pastor Bryan and Lynn were in a serious motorcycle accident. We are saddened that Lynn passed away as a result of injuries sustained during the accident.

Bryan underwent surgery and remains hospitalized. As updates on his condition become available, they will be shared on our GT website and GT social media channels. Please continue to respect the privacy of the family during this difficult time.

Please pray specifically for healing for Bryan and peace and comfort for the family.

The GT Worship Center in West Lawn will be open today beginning at 9 am for prayer.

Thank you,

The GT Staff

Psalm 34:18 (NLT)

The Lord is close to the brokenhearted; He rescues those whose spirits are crushed.

When they hit send, the weight that had already settled on the atrium became heavier. Writing that email somehow made everything feel final. It had all really happened and there was no turning back now. People slowly started to head home, and eventually the church was empty and quiet once again, but not for long. Just four hours later it would begin to fill with the sunlight of a new day.

Steve Pennington was in Springfield, Missouri, when his phone rang late on the evening of June 7. It was the regional director for the Assemblies of God World Missions in Africa. Steve and his wife, Trina, lived in Africa, but happened to be home getting ready to train new missionaries before they headed out to the field. He picked up his phone.

"Steve, have you heard about Bryan?" his friend asked on the other end.

"No...what's up?" Steve replied, confused. It was a vague question and odd timing.

There was a slight pause before he heard, "Well, there's been an accident. Bryan's not doing too good."

Steve's breath caught in his throat, "Well you know..."

"Yes, I do know," his friend replied, cutting him off, "get on a plane and get up there."

Steve hung up the phone and sat for a moment. Bryan was one of his oldest and dearest friends. They were like brothers, their families were close, and they had known one another for what felt like a lifetime. Steve filled his wife in on what he knew, and she immediately booked him a plane ticket for the earliest flight she could get, Tuesday morning. Steve started scrolling through his phone, trying to figure out where to get more info, but the only numbers he had were for Bryan, Lynn, and the church. They went to bed, but Steve couldn't find sleep.

Back in Reading, at the hospital, the family was just starting to head home to get a few hours of sleep before they needed to return to face the next day. There was nothing they could do for Bryan except pray, and Monday morning would bring its own worries and decisions. The three Koch boys and Jen pulled up to Bryan's house and sat for a moment before getting out of the car. None of them were quite sure that they were ready to walk into the house. There was complete silence as they turned the doorknob and stepped into the dark foyer; the house had an eerie emptiness to it and the reality of the night's events descended on them. The four said nothing and just walked to their separate rooms, where they each sat on their own beds, quietly crying tears of grief, unbelief, and utter sadness.

At the hospital they had been met with medical decisions and information, but here there was nothing but silence, and the silence was heavy. Everywhere they looked they were met with reminders of their parents and a life that, just hours ago, was perfectly intact. But now it was all broken. Each of them lay in bed that night, willing their bodies to accept the sleep they so desperately needed, but unable to give in to sleep.

Five o'clock came quickly, and the sound of Ben's alarm pierced the quiet morning. "Time to get up," he said as he walked into his brothers' rooms. They all dressed and headed back to the hospital—to the start of a new day, a new life, and a new routine.

They walked back into the hospital and into the

ICU conference room, where the family started to gather. Bryan's parents, Donna and Ted, Ronda, Renee, and their husbands were all weary from a restless night of replaying Sunday's events over and over in their heads.

They had no words for one another. Nothing any of them could say would make the whole situation go away, and so they sat there quietly until the surgeon walked in and said, "Well, we have good news. Bryan made it through the night."

"That's good!" Ronda thought to herself.

And then the surgeon began detailing the surgeries ahead, listing all of the things that could go wrong, and ending with, "...and if that happens, there's nothing we can do."

"There's nothing we can do" sounds like a line that is reserved for movie scripts and television dramas, not real life. As the family listened to all that could go wrong, it seemed unthinkable that a problem could arise that modern medicine wouldn't be able to fix. If Bryan had survived the accident, surely it wasn't just so that he could die in the hospital of an infection. Seated next to Ronda, Donna buried her head in her hands and started crying.

Ronda just wanted the doctor to stop talking. He seemed to go on and on, and with every word the weight of the medical information got heavier and heavier. Couldn't they just cling to the good news he started with?

As the surgeon worked his way down Bryan's chart, he eventually got to his leg. The surgical team had removed Bryan's left leg above his knee the night before due to injuries, and care of his leg would be an important part of his recovery. He walked them through the three stages of trauma: survival, respiratory function, and infection; three words that would mark the rest of Bryan's immediate recovery. And before he left the room, he asked Ben to sign forms authorizing the next surgery that Bryan would have that day.

Meanwhile in Ohio, Bryan's sister, Marsha, was just getting on the road to drive to Pennsylvania. She had gotten the call the night before around nine thirty, and had spent the evening getting things lined up with work and her life group, who had offered to step in to take care of her home while she was gone. She had tried in vain to sleep and was up with the sun, ready to get on the road early the next day to make the nearly eight-hour drive to Reading. As she started her drive, she put on worship music and began to pray her way across Pennsylvania.

At eight o'clock, the GT staff gathered together for an update. There was something comforting about all being in the same room with a spirit of comradery as they all came together. In an hour the doors of the church would be open for prayer, and the staff took that first hour together to begin working through what their roles would be over the next few days. It felt as if life had come to a crashing halt, but the reality remained that Sunday was coming, and no one yet knew what that would mean for the church.

Everyone did their best to put on a brave face that Monday, but in the back of their minds, no one could shake the constant worry that Bryan might not make it. His injuries were severe and hearing the reports from the doctors brought little comfort. It seemed that with each new surgery or procedure there were more concerning potential side effects. Bryan's body was swollen and had tubes and wires protruding from it. There were surgeries to fix things in his abdomen, surgeries to stop blood clots from getting to his heart, surgeries to address infection in his leg. For the first four days after the accident, his life was left hanging in the balance.

Everyone was left in a state of uncertainty as to whether their dad, brother, son, pastor, and friend would ever wake up again.

Chapter 5

Left Lives

June 2015

Always be full of joy in the Lord. I say it again – rejoice!
Let everyone see that you are considerate in all you do.
Remember, the Lord is coming soon.
Philippians 4:4 (NLT)

Steve Pennington landed in Harrisburg, Pennsylvania, on the morning of Tuesday, June 9. By then, he had been in contact with some of GT's staff and had some information. He rented a car and, not really knowing where to go, drove straight to the church.

That day, the church was filled with people praying. The community came and went throughout the day, spending time praying in and around the building, waiting for any word or update on Bryan. Steve was standing in the back of the Worship Center when one of GT's pastors came up to him. The two had met earlier that year in Africa, and Steve was grateful for a familiar face.

"You probably want to see Bryan, don't you?" It was more of a statement than a question.

Steve exhaled, "I really do."

They got in the car, a sad silence between them. As they pulled up to the hospital, Steve closed his eyes and prayed, bracing himself for what he was about to walk into, and asking God to show him how he could help.

After greeting the family, Steve went in to see Bryan. Like others before him, he got choked up looking at his friend lying helplessly in the hospital bed. Emerging from the ICU room, he was met by the pastor that drove him to the hospital. "You know, the boys would really like you to stay at the house." And immediately, Steve knew why God had brought him to Reading.

Ben and Jen had temporarily moved into the Koch house with Brett and Bryce, and the four of them were all trying to balance taking care of the house and spending long hours at the hospital. Steve moving in was a breath of fresh air. He brought them some sense of normalcy and guidance. He was like a light in the midst of the darkness. He was goofy like Bryan, and joked with them like a dad. He cooked them breakfast and had conversations with each of them to check in on how they were doing. Not long after Steve arrived, his wife, Trina, followed and she dove right into caring for the house, taking that concern off of Ronda and Renee. Their presence was a blessing to the whole family.

When Marsha arrived, she quickly became the point person for all things medical, assisting Ben as he made decisions about his dad's care. Her background in pharmaceuticals gave her an understanding of medical terms, and she got to the hospital each morning as the doctors were doing their rounds so that she could get the day's update on Bryan's condition and status and report back to the rest of the family.

Both Steve and Marsha played crucial roles in the first few weeks following the accident, and they both left lives behind to come to Bryan's side. It was amazing how the community rallied around the Koch family. People across the world followed GT's social media accounts and looked for updates on Bryan. Churches in Africa were praying for him nightly at their meetings. The prayers of thousands of people were being felt in Reading, Pennsylvania.

Wednesday night, just three days after the accident, GT held a prayer service. The church was packed. The fifteen-hundred-seat Worship Center was filled to capacity and seating overflowed into other spaces on GT's campus. The church building was bursting with people from all over the community coming to pray. Reporters from local media outlets were covering the evening, other churches were represented, and people who had never before set foot inside of GT Church showed up to offer their support.

After some worship, Scott Kramer took the stage. As GT's Executive Pastor, he had been put into the role of leader. GT's Elder Board lined the stage behind him. "Our church family has seen the most unthinkable events that this church has ever seen. We have people joining us from all different churches tonight. The expressions of love and care and support and prayer have been overwhelming to this church, to our staff, and to our family. This is a time that our church family is banding together."

Scott paused for a moment as scattered applause rang around the room. "You might be visiting with us tonight. Some might think it's strange that we start a night like this with worship, but I've been meditating on Philippians chapter four the past few days, and it says, 'Rejoice in all things, again I say rejoice! Let your gentleness be evident to all; the

Lord is near.' What we are facing as a church family has not surprised God, and God is near. He's near to us in this place, he's near to Bryan in the hospital room. And he's near to the family and near to your heart. And we are just overwhelmed by the outpouring of love here tonight."

The night continued with the elders leading the church in prayer, and giving updates on Bryan and how the church was going to proceed. Questions had been hanging in the air the past few days: Would the church continue on with its summer calendar? What decision would be most honoring to Lynn?

After more worship, one of the GT elders stepped to the center of the stage. "There are big questions that come up when something like this happens. Why did this happen? What do we do now? What possibly could we do now? What do we lay down? What do we pick up? What do we have to hope in? But they that hope in the Lord will renew their strength. We need to run and not be weary, we need to walk and not faint. So we wanted you to know that we've been grappling with these questions. Life just doesn't go on as normal. This isn't just life as usual, except there are some things that remain as constant. And we said what would Bryan want us to do as a church? He would say move forward. He would say move forward into this community and this nation and this world. We have a team leaving Monday morning for Uganda, for a place that was on our pastor's heart. And so, do we go?"

Voices called out a resounding "yes" from around the room.

"Our pastor would want us to go to Uganda, because people in Uganda need Jesus, they need hope. We have a big week coming up at GT. It's called Vacation Bible School. It's called Extreme Vacation Bible School. And so we ask, can we have a VBS just days after we lay the body of our pastor's wife in the ground? We had to sit back and ask that question. Can we do that? We began to pray and ask God for direction on that. There's a balance between pausing and remembering and moving forward. And when it came down to it, we recognized that Lynn's heart would say that kids still need Jesus. And people might say, 'How can they celebrate when such tragedy has come?' But we don't do it in spite of, we do it to honor the very heart of Lynn Koch, who's worked at VBS, who cared for children. So we are moving forward with VBS because it would be Lynn's heart to do this. We do VBS because kids need Jesus. We are keeping VBS because it reflects the heart of Lynn Koch for kids."

Cheers rang throughout the room; amidst tears and heartache, there would still be joy and hope that could only come from Jesus Christ. And move forward they did. Even in the felt loss of Bryan and Lynn on the GT community, the staff and elders of GT knew that people still needed to hear about Jesus, and so they honored their pastor and his wife by carrying on the mission and vision of GT through the deepest season of grief the church had ever known.

June 14, 2015: Bryan's boys being prayed for by GT elders one week after the accident. The boys also addressed the congregation. (Pictured left to right: Bryce, Brett, Ben, Jen.) Photo courtesy of GT Church.

As the initial shock of the accident started to dull, the family began the arduous task of planning Lynn's funeral. It was agonizing to be making decisions without Bryan, and all any of them really wanted was to be able to talk to him. They took turns sitting at his bedside and waiting in the conference room the hospital had assigned to them as he was taken in and out of surgeries and procedures. They worked out a schedule of who would be there each hour of the day. Each day would start off with Greg, one of GT's elders and Bryan's closest friends, sitting in the chair next to his bed, talking to him, reading Scripture, and praying. Meanwhile, Donna filled Bryan's hospital room with Scripture and music. She prayed her son through some of his darkest days, and literally surrounded him with the Word of God.

The next week was filled with meetings - meetings with doctors and funeral directors, pastors and social workers. Lynn hated funerals, and the last thing she would have wanted was to be put on display. She wanted nothing to do with hearses and never liked funeral processions or big services. The family really wanted to keep things small and quiet and private, and for the most part, the public really respected those wishes.

A week and a half after the accident, the family arrived at the church early in the morning, dressed in black and as mentally prepared as possible for what would be one of the hardest days of their lives. The funeral directors set up the casket at the front of the room where the private funeral was to be held, and one by one, the family took their turns saying goodbye to the mother, sister, daughter, and friend that they had all loved and now missed dearly.

As the room started to fill with GT's staff and Bryan and Lynn's extended families, the casket was closed. The rest of the day was a bit of a blur, with internment and a large reception to follow. Though there was obvious pain throughout the whole process, there was also fond laughter as friends and family remembered all of the good and goofy moments they had had with Lynn. At the luncheon following the funeral, everyone honored Lynn with her favorite treat, ice cream.

One of the biggest stresses of the day, however, was the news that was breaking as the family was saying goodbye to Lynn. Ben had gotten a call from the police the day before, letting him know that the investigation of the accident had revealed that the fault lay with the driver of the other vehicle that was involved. He had been intoxicated, more than four times the legal limit in fact, when he lost control of his car and crossed the center line of the road, hitting Bryan and Lynn. The news broke early Wednesday morning, and the family did their best to ignore the newspaper articles that were being shared left and right on social media.

That evening, GT held Celebration of Life services for the community to come and pay their respects. Overall, it was an exhausting day, and it wasn't over as the family once again headed back to the hospital.

Chapter 6

Left Alone

Summer 2015

For to me, to live is Christ and to die is gain.
Philippians 1:21 (NIV)

After Lynn's funeral, Bryan's recovery started progressing quickly. The day after the funeral, eleven days after the accident, Bryan's medical team started weaning him off of his sedation medication. It would take a few days before Bryan was fully out of the sedation, but each day the family could see him fighting it and gaining more consciousness. Greg and Ben took turns sleeping at the hospital each night because as the sedation medicine began to wear off, Bryan started becoming agitated by his feeding and breathing tubes. He certainly hadn't lost his strength, and it took a careful watch on him to keep him from pulling out the tubes and wires he was hooked up to.

Each day, the nurses would write goals on his whiteboard. "Open eyes" or "squeeze hands" they read. Little goals to most people, but big ones for Bryan.

The hospital social workers had coached them through the hardest conversations they'd have to have with Bryan. They were told to be very direct. When Bryan asked where Lynn was, they were to be clear and say, "She died." Anything else could end up confusing him. They had to speak the words that had been so hard for so long. No saying "she's with Jesus" or "she passed;" they needed to be clear and direct.

As Bryan came out of the sedation he started asking the questions the social workers said he would. It took him a while to even remember who everyone was, and even longer to remember where he was from day to day, and why he was in the hospital. This made for a lot of repeat conversations. Each family member had their own encounter with him asking questions about the accident and Lynn, and each encounter was similar.

One day Ben was sitting on Bryan's left and Ronda and Renee were on his right. He had been getting clearer by the day and they could tell by the look on his face that he knew something was up. "You guys know something..." he said cautiously.

Ronda, Renee, and Ben shared a glance, silently deciding which one of them would be the one to say it. Ronda spoke first, "Bryan, Lynn is dead."

"Oh...oh...how'd that happen?" Bryan said, visibly confused and trying to process.

"Dad, there was an accident on your bike." Ben started filling in some of the gaps as Bryan was connecting the dots. Ronda immediately started texting Marsha to let her know he was asking questions. But not every answer to those questions stuck, and those were questions that would be asked again.

By June 21, two full weeks after the accident, Bryan was eating and was having good and bad days. He was most peaceful when worship music was playing in his room, and would even worship in tongues. But other days he was agitated, ripping out his IV's. He was also fearful from time to time, waking from nightmares that he was in the midst of a war, only to look down and see half of his leg missing. The mix of medications and trauma were taking a toll on his mind, and he started having restless nights, fighting with the mittens that the nurses placed on his hands to keep him from pulling out his cords and tubes, and having moments of confusion in the middle of the dark nights in the hospital.

As Bryan became more alert, bits and pieces of his personality began to come back and shine through. When the nurses would deliver his medicine, they'd ask him for his name and birthdate. Bryan would often answer their question and tag on, "And I'm born again," and give some spiritual identification to his life at the end. He also started thanking the nurses for their ministry while in the hospital. Some nurses laughed those little nuances off, but one nurse in particular really took Bryan's case to heart.

One night, while he was standing in the doorway of his room watching him sleep, she approached Steve. "Are you the guy from Africa?" she whispered.

"Yeah, that's me," he replied.

"I'm from GT. I just wanted you to know...when he leaves here...when he walks out of here...he's my pastor. He's my assignment." Whenever she entered Bryan's room, prayer wasn't far from her lips. And it was clear that God was ministering to Bryan through more than just the family gathered at his bedside.

By June 27, the doctors were starting to feel optimistic about Bryan's leg. He had come through the survival and respiratory stages of trauma, and their biggest concern and focus had shifted from his lungs and internal organs and onto his leg. The possibility of infection was high, but they were diligent in cleaning and monitoring what residual leg he had left. As June began to come to a close, the doctors started to feel like his leg was moving in the right direction and moved him from the intensive care unit to a regular nursing unit in the hospital.

Being at the hospital around the clock was becoming exhausting for the family, so once Bryan moved from the ICU, they created a schedule and took two-hour shifts. Someone was with Bryan all day, and at night the hospital assigned someone to keep watch on his room in case he woke in a panic or confusion.

A week later, on July 8, Bryan saw the outside of a hospital room for the first time in a month. He got his cell phone back and started communicating with his family via text. Marsha had consulted with doctors and had agreed that his phone time needed to be limited, so she removed anything work-related from it. This, in particular, frustrated Bryan, as he was getting more and more curious about what was going on back at GT.

On July 27, almost two months after his accident, Bryan left the Reading Hospital and moved to the Reading Hospital's inpatient rehabilitation center. He started a rigorous schedule of speech, physical, and occupational therapy as he learned to navigate the world with only half of a leg, learning how to move in a wheelchair and how to transition from his chair to a bed.

He was at the rehab hospital for ten days before heading home on August 7, to a house filled with family and a big "Welcome Home Bryan" sign hung above his garage. Steve and Trina Pennington had left weeks earlier and Ben and Jen had moved back to their own home. Marsha had moved into the house so that Brett and Bryce wouldn't be there alone, and also so that she could help get things ready for Bryan's return.

August 7, 2015: Bryan returns home one day before his
28th wedding anniversary.
Photo courtesy of Marsha Koch.

August 8 would have been Bryan and Lynn's wedding anniversary, and was one of the hardest days Bryan had had thus far in his recovery. Being in a home that the two of them had shared for so long was difficult, and facing an anniversary without his wife was painful. The business of rehab had kept him focused on recovery without much time to think about life without his wife, and now that he was home, the loss was more evident than ever. It wasn't until he was back in his home that he really felt like he had been left alone. Sure, he was surrounded by people who were doing everything they could to help him heal physically, but no one could help him heal emotionally. That, he needed to do on his own, with help from God.

As life started to return to normal for the family, Bryan got into a rhythm of therapy, adjusting to his new life, and getting back into work. He had filmed a short greeting video to the staff when he was still in the hospital, but in late August, he decided to stop by GT. News that Bryan was there spread quickly throughout the building and soon the whole staff was gathered in the youth worship center, chairs pulled around Bryan, who was sitting in his wheelchair. Pure joy was coursing through the room as the staff beamed at their pastor and leader, excited that he was there in front of them. Bryan spoke for a while about his recovery and what God was doing through all of it, and it seemed like the afternoon just stopped. The staff of GT Church had really clung to one another that summer, and to be sitting in a room with Bryan back was the culmination of so many prayers that had been offered up.

He slowly started getting back into work. He held meetings at his home, started coming into the office for a few hours a week, and tuned in every week to watch church online. Eventually, a date was set for his official return to the GT stage. The fall teaching series was to be titled "EPIC," a six-week series detailing six of the more "epic" stories in the Bible, including David and Goliath, Noah's ark, and Moses parting the Red Sea. The service planning team had planned all of it out earlier that spring, not yet knowing the epic events that the summer of 2015 would hold. And so it was decided that Bryan would make an epic return on October 18.

Chapter 7

Left Standing

October 18, 2015

*For I am about to do something new. See, I have
already begun! Do you not see it? I will make a path-
way through the wilderness. I will create rivers in the
dry wasteland.*
Isaiah 43:19 (NLT)

The buzz leading up to October 18 was palpable. From
the moment GT started announcing Bryan's return,
people began inviting their friends and family to be
there on the first day that he would stand on the GT
stage since his accident.

Bryan was excited to get back to his church and
started diving back into work at his normal pace.
His doctors had started weaning him off of some of
his medication at the end of August, and by October
he was making big strides in his recovery. He was

finally able to transition from his wheelchair to his walker on his own.

Bryan felt like he was in a movie. It was almost as if he didn't know who he was anymore; like he needed to introduce himself to himself again. He knew that he wasn't the same Bryan Koch that he had been for fifty-two years. Processing through all that had happened would just take some time.

When he was in rehab, one of his final therapy sessions had included him writing a sermon. He was just supposed to give an overview of it to his therapists, but he ended up standing and delivering the entire thing in the rehab hospital's small chapel. As October 18 neared, he took that sermon and worked on it for his return.

Expecting a large crowd, the GT staff decided that it would be best to hold an additional evening service that Sunday, bringing the total service count to three for that day. Special invitations were sent to first responders and Bryan's medical team. Seats were reserved in the front rows for these guests and family.

When October 18 rolled around, Bryan was nervous. He hadn't been nervous to preach in years. Things were different this time, though. He had walked onto the GT stage countless times, but this time, he'd have a lot more to think about than ever before. To begin with, he'd be rolling himself out on the stage in a wheelchair. He'd also be doing his best to stand throughout the sermon. He'd have to put all that he'd learned in therapy into action, while at the same time trying not to get too emotional over being back with his church for the first time in over four months.

The service began with worship. There was an air of expectation and complete adoration for God that morning. The congregation knew what was coming, and the excitement built along with the worship music.

As worship wound down, Scott Kramer walked out on stage to welcome everyone to church that morning. He gave a few announcements and prayed over the offering, and then the room went dark. The screens flanking each side of the stage lit up with white text that simply read: "The Lord is close to the brokenhearted; he rescues those whose spirits are crushed. -Psalm 34:18"

The screens went dark again, and as music started to play, text scrolled that read: "On the morning of June 7, 2015, GT Church honored first responders for all they do to serve our community." Images of the American flag and fire trucks filled the screen, along with images of GT's first responders services.

Then, more text: "Later that evening, some of those very first responders we honored responded to a call that would change many lives forever…"

The screens went black again, as Ronda's voice played in the darkness: "At 6pm that evening, Pastors Bryan and Lynn were in a tragic accident. As a result of that accident, Pastor Bryan lost both his leg and his wife of twenty-eight years."

As the screen began flashing images of the accident scene, a news report played along with a voice-over: "An urgent prayer request has been issued to the members of GT Church in Spring Township after one of its pastors was killed and another seriously injured in a motorcycle crash around six Sunday night. Pastor Bryan Koch and his wife, Lynn Koch, were riding southbound on a motorcycle together on Grange Road in Bern Township when police say a northbound SUV struck them in the southbound lane. Pastor Lynn was killed; Pastor Bryan was flown to Reading Hospital where he is reportedly recovering from abdominal injuries and a leg amputation."

Footage of people pouring into the church in June filled the screen as Ronda's voice was heard again: "Immediately, our church family, the community, and people from around the world began to pray."

Clips from the prayer services just days after Bryan's accident rolled, with Scott, Steve, and Greg all encouraging the church congregation and providing vision and comfort in the midst of tragedy, and then, Ronda's voice one more time...

"Saying goodbye to our beloved friend, sister, daughter, mother, and soon-to-be grandmother and pastor was difficult, but as Pastor Greg shared at Lynn's services, we all rejoiced in knowing that she was the only person who wasn't hurting. She is now in the presence of Jesus. Lynn was a humble servant who truly loved to serve behind the scenes in areas that were important to her.

"She had a tremendous love for children, and it was an honor to move forward with our annual Vacation Bible School this summer, and it was in recognition of her desire to see children come to know Jesus. She also was very passionate about encouraging and equipping other women. Lynn had recently led a team to Romania on a missions trip, and as a tribute to her, our PennDel Network is donating over $150,000 for a ministry center to be built in the same city she visited on her trip this past February.

In the weeks to follow, our entire church family celebrated each step in Pastor Bryan's miraculous recovery..."

Photos of Bryan along the road of his recovery flashed and ended with one slide...

"17 surgeries,

36 units of blood,

51 days in the hospital,

Over 6,000 cards received,

An infinite number of prayers.

Today is an EPIC day in the life of our church.

After 19 weeks...please welcome back Pastor Bryan!"

Bryan went rolling out onto the stage, tears streaming down his face, as the congregation stood with thundering applause. Standing behind his walker, he pointed heavenward saying, "We give you praise, God."

He went on to preach a sermon which will be remembered forever. He could have spoken about anything he wanted, but he decided to stick with the planned theme of the day and preached on Moses. He brought his whole family out on stage, including his four-day-old grandson, Jackson, and then he went on to talk about how God parted the waters for Moses and the Israelites to walk right through.

In the hospital, Bryan's niece had written him a card that had hung on the wall of his room. It read, "If God brings you to it, He'll bring you through it." That became an anthem for Bryan, and he wove his story together with Moses's, talking about the seemingly impossible and unthinkable situations they were both in, and how God made a way when there seemed to be none.

GT's services on October 18 were broadcast around the globe. Everyone rejoiced at seeing the man that they had prayed for on the stage where he belonged once again. Bryan was back, and he was ready to be a vessel for God in a way he had never been before.

But Bryan was no stranger to God using his life's circumstances for His glory.

October 18, 2015: Bryan's first day back, 133 days after the accident. Photo courtesy of GT Church.

October 18, 2015: Bryan's family joins him to celebrate his return to the GT stage. Photo courtesy of GT Church.

Chapter 8

Left Shaken

1981

This is what the Lord says:
"Cursed is the one who trusts in man,
who draws strength from mere flesh
and whose heart turns away from the Lord.
That person will be like a bush in the wastelands;
they will not see prosperity when it comes.
They will dwell in the parched places of the desert,
in a salt land where no one lives.
But blessed is the one who trusts in the Lord,
whose confidence is in him.
They will be like a tree planted by the water
that sends out its roots by the stream.
It does not fear when heat comes;
its leaves are always green.
It has no worries in a year of drought
and never fails to bear fruit."
Jeremiah 17:5-8 (NIV)

"Bryan, get in the van." Fifteen-year-old Bryan Koch was leaving work one night when two of his coworkers pulled up in one of the company vans. They could all be described as young adults, doing crazy stuff and getting into trouble from time to time, but that night was different than most. Bryan climbed in the van.

"Where are we going?"

"Just sit down, we have something to do," said one of the guys.

They drove down some back roads until they came to a field. The farmland seemed to sparkle in the early moonlight, frost beginning to set in, and they pulled the van just off of the road.

"Get out and give us a hand." Bryan did as he was told, following his coworkers into the field. They walked until they came upon a snowplow, and Bryan watched as his two coworkers motioned for him to grab a corner of it. The three of them carried it back to the van, where they loaded it into the open back doors. Left without a seat, Bryan perched on the front of the plow as they closed the door and started to drive off over bumpy farm roads.

The van started careening down a hill, gaining more and more speed and falling more and more out of control. Finally, it came to an abrupt halt as the front end slammed into a tree. Bryan, still perched on the plow, lurched forward, his face making contact with the dashboard. He pushed himself back, glasses askew, and as he took them off of his face, he realized that they had broken in the collision and he was bleeding from somewhere on his head.

The three of them got out of the van to examine the damage. "Get out of here, Bryan," muttered one of his co-workers, as the other climbed back into the van to back it off of the tree, "Just get out of here and walk home."

Still shaking, Bryan looked at the scene in front of him, thinking all the while about how he had gotten himself into this situation and just how angry his dad was going to be when he got home. And then he turned around and started to walk down the dark road.

Bryan had a reputation at Muhlenberg High School. He was a great athlete and one of the stars of the baseball team, but a very average student. He rarely studied, made grades just good enough to keep himself out of trouble with his coaches, and focused on his passion, baseball. He partied and drank at friends' houses on the weekends. But he came from a hard-working family, and he, his sister, and his parents went to a local Lutheran church on

Christmas, Easter, and every so often in between. For the most part, Bryan kept out of any real trouble, except for the occasional event like that night in the van.

In the spring of his junior year of high school, Bryan found himself in the library. As he sat at a table, bored with the work in front of him, his gaze drifted across the room to a girl who was sitting bent over her notebook, scribbling furiously as she took notes from an open textbook lying next to her. She had her hair gathered up in a bun and kept pushing her glasses up as they slid down her nose. For some reason that day, Bryan was intrigued by her. She was pretty and he wondered why he hadn't noticed her before. He stood up, walked across the library, and confidently approached her table.

"Hey...I'm Bryan," he said as he took the seat across from her, "what are you working on?"

"Hi...I'm Liz."

The two began to chat, Bryan charming Liz as he told jokes and she tried to stifle giggles in the quiet library. It was the unlikeliest of pairings, but the two quickly became close. One night, Liz invited Bryan home with her to meet her parents. Nervous yet trying to keep his cool, Bryan agreed to go over for dinner.

"So, you're interested in spending time with my daughter?" Liz's father asked Bryan.

"Yes, sir," Bryan replied, trying to convince the man looking skeptically at him that he was, in fact, one of the good guys.

"Well that's fine, but there's one condition. The only place you can go with Liz is to church."

Bryan stammered, "Um...ok..." but internally he was thinking, "Church?! I can only take her to church?"

But Bryan liked Liz, so he went to church. He went to church on Sundays and on Wednesdays with Liz's family and then one Tuesday night, Liz invited him to a revival service. She was singing in a chorus with other teenagers from the youth group and asked Bryan to come hear them sing. Not wanting to miss another opportunity to see the girl he liked, he agreed to go. Bryan showed up that night figuring that he would sit in a service, sing some songs, hear a sermon, and then hang out with Liz and her friends, and go home by curfew.

He showed up at the Nazarene church and took his seat in a pew next to Liz and her friends. After some music, an older preacher took the pulpit and began his message. Something about his sermon that night left Bryan enraptured. As the preacher spoke about heaven and hell, Bryan began to feel more and more convicted. At first, he tried to brush off what he was feeling, but soon he couldn't escape the work that the Holy Spirit was doing inside of him.

"I'm a sinner," he thought sitting in his seat in the pew listening to the preacher describe the fate of people who don't know Jesus. "I'm a sinner, and I am lost."

The worship leader came back up and led the congregation in a hymn. Bryan felt like he was jumping out of his own skin. He just wanted to get out of there, and fast. But sitting there, sandwiched in the middle of the other teenagers in the youth group, there was no way for him to escape without making a scene. As the hymn came to a close, the preacher stepped back onto the stage. He began to explain that salvation was offered free to everyone through belief in Jesus, and all anyone had to do was to pray and ask for it. And as he asked for those who wanted to receive Christ to raise their hand, Bryan felt his hand go up in the air.

The preacher asked those with their hands in the air to come forward to the front of the church, and without a second thought, Bryan went. He had never done anything like it in his life, and he had never experienced such strong conviction over anything.

Shaking, he made his way toward the altar, where a man met him to lead him through the prayer of salvation. As Bryan asked Christ to be his savior, hot tears rolled down his cheeks. The cool baseball player with a tough reputation stood there, bawling, overwhelmed by the urging of the Holy Spirit and the love of Jesus.

The worship music swelled and quieted and the preacher invited Bryan to come up onto the stage to tell everyone about his decision to follow Christ. For the first of what would be countless times in his life, Bryan stepped up in front of a room full of people in a church. But that night, he couldn't find the right words to describe what he was feeling. In truth, he didn't know *what* had happened to him, but he knew something was different. He was left shaken by the experience.

The man who had prayed with Bryan told him that he needed to do three things: read his Bible, pray, and go to church. And as Bryan left the church, he decided that he would do all of those things.

Bryan arrived at home that night much like he had months earlier when he had been in the accident with his friends from work. Except this time, instead of coming home to an angry dad, he came home to a worried mom. He walked into the house, turned on the light, and was startled to find her waiting there for him.

"Bryan, where in the world were you? It's a school night," she said.

"Mom, I was at church," he replied calmly, still reeling from what he had experienced.

"All right Bryan, I'm going to ask you one more time, and this time you better tell me the truth or I'm getting your father. Where were you?" Donna asked again, still not sure that her son would spend his Tuesday night at a church of all places.

"Mom, I am telling you the truth. I was at church with Liz and her family. And Mom, I need to tell you something."

Bryan spent the next few minutes explaining to his mom what had happened to him that night. He told her how he went to the church just to spend more time with Liz, but he ended up experiencing Jesus in a way he never had before. He explained to her what the preacher had said about how the only way to go to heaven was by accepting Christ and how, when he stood up at the front of the church and asked if anyone wanted to make that decision, Bryan's hand had popped up in the air. As he described the conviction he felt and how he cried when he prayed the prayer of salvation, Donna began to cry.

She got down on her knees right there in front of Bryan in the living room, and on that night in 1981 dedicated her life to serving Jesus.

Donna started going to church with Bryan. He took her to a revival meeting, she started watching evangelists on television, and she clung to her new faith with everything she had. Bryan spent his evenings at church or youth group and he prayed and he read his Bible, just like he had been told to that night at the revival meeting. One evening not long after he got saved, he was sitting at home reading from Zechariah and he thought, "Man, this guy has more problems than I do." The more Bryan read and spent time at church, the more convicted he felt. He stopped partying, stopped hanging out with his old friends, and slowly but surely, his life began to change.

As he entered his senior year in the fall of 1981, Bryan was sharing his faith with others at school. He was attending youth group with Liz and her friends, spending Sundays and Wednesdays at the Nazarene church. His sister, Marsha, got saved and his family was going to church faithfully. It looked like Bryan's life was turning around for the better, and he started focusing on his baseball career more than ever.

Chapter 9

Left Eye

1982-1985

The wise prevail through great power,
and those who have knowledge muster their strength.
Proverbs 24:5 (NIV)

By the spring of 1982, Bryan's faith had started to grow. His reputation at school began to change as he shared his newfound faith with others, went to church regularly, and started hanging out with a different crowd. As he approached his eighteenth birthday and graduation, he started to think about his future. He had received an invitation to play baseball at Arizona State, but what he really wanted to do was play professional baseball.

That year, Bryan's team at Muhlenberg High School had an all-star pitcher. Scouts began to show up to games to see this kid play. At one particular game, a scout for the Toronto Blue Jays had shown up to see Bryan's teammate. As it turned out, Bryan had a great game, and at the end of it the scout walked up to him and asked him if he'd ever considered playing professional ball.

Considered it? Bryan dreamed of it! It was all he had ever wanted. The Blue Jays registered Bryan into the draft system and he began getting letters in the mail from other teams who were interested in him. The California Angels, St. Louis Cardinals...to a seventeen-year-old high school kid, this was like living a fantasy. Major League teams knew his name!

In May, Bryan turned eighteen, and then a few weeks later on a Thursday night, he walked across the Muhlenberg High School stage and received his diploma. On Friday, Bryan got a phone call that he had been drafted by the Chicago White Sox organization. And on Monday, Bryan was in the backseat of his parents' car driving to the airport to head to rookie ball in Sarasota, Florida.

Bryan fiddled with his bag in the backseat. He was nervous. Everything had happened so quickly and here he was, about to embark on the adventure of his life at only eighteen. The anticipation of what laid before him was almost overwhelming.

He got on the airplane, determined to relax on the flight before arriving in Sarasota, but all he could think of was his dad. Ted had always been a hard-working guy and a good father. Even though Donna had gotten saved the year before and she and Bryan's sister, Marsha, were faithfully following Jesus, Ted hadn't bought into the whole faith thing yet. Somewhere over North Carolina, Bryan decided that he'd focus on praying for his dad during his time in Florida.

A few weeks after his arrival in Florida, Bryan was still feeling a burden in his spirit for his dad. He was praying daily for him, but he felt God pushing him to do something more. So one night, Bryan sat down and started writing. He wrote about how his dad was a good father, a hard worker, a great example. And he wrote about how all of that was good, but it wouldn't get him into heaven. That week, Bryan sent his dad a ten-page letter in the mail, explaining how much he desired to see his dad come to know Jesus.

When the thick envelope arrived at Ted and Donna's house, Donna thought that it must be an update from Bryan, and she opened it up, expecting to find news of his first year playing professional baseball. Instead, she found a heartfelt letter from her son to his father. After reading all ten pages, Donna went into her bedroom and prayed. She prayed all afternoon until her husband came home from his eleven-hour shift at the concrete plant, and when he sat down to dinner, she placed the letter in front of him.

Ted sat and quietly read. And as he read, the tears started to fall from his eyes. Looking up at Donna, he admitted that he was finally ready to receive Christ. Hearing her husband utter those words made Donna's eyes well up with tears. Somehow that night she found a church that was holding a service and the two of them went. Ted prayed and accepted Christ, and that same night Donna wrote a simple letter back to her son that read, "Praise the Lord! Your dad got saved!"

Bryan spent the summer of 1982 playing rookie ball in Sarasota. By the time he joined the White Sox organization in June, spring training was over, and he was put in a rookie league, where he went from being a high school all star to sitting second to the White Sox's first draft pick, who was also a catcher. The summer was exciting, yet uneventful, and when rookie ball was over, Bryan moved back home to Reading.

That fall, Bryan decided that he might as well spend the off-season working toward his future, in case the whole baseball thing didn't work out. He began attending Kutztown University and took two classes. And just like in high school, he was a bad student in college.

He also spent the next school year working. He got a job at UPS, getting up at two o'clock in the morning each day and putting packages on the trucks for delivery. Bryan hated that job. His boss had played baseball for a rival high school and the two didn't see eye-to-eye, so between that dynamic and the fact that he had to be up early each day, Bryan spent most days at work wanting to quit. But he stuck it out until a few weeks before spring training began.

In the early spring, Bryan left Reading and headed to Fresno, California. One of his buddies from rookie ball was living out there with his family and he was a pitcher, so Bryan spent a couple of weeks warming up for the season with his friend. On his first Sunday in California, Bryan went along to church with his friend's family. That day was the first time he stepped foot in an Assemblies of God church, and Bryan was freaked out by it. It was a far cry from his Nazarene church back home.

Bryan and his friend flew to Sarasota to spend the 1983 season on Siesta Key. That summer, Bryan got to play most of the games that his minor league team played, and he spent that summer gaining the attention of his coaches and growing in his technique. He headed home feeling like his summer of hard work was going to pay off, and he spent the next year working again.

By the time spring of 1985 rolled around, Bryan had hit his stride. He was older, he was bigger, and three years of rookie ball had turned him into a good, defensive catcher with a good arm. He hustled at practice and his coaches liked his attitude. Once again, he returned to Florida to gear up for another season of playing eight-hour days of baseball.

Spring training prior to a career-ending injury.
Photo courtesy of the family.

Living in Sarasota, the team put players in condos a few miles from the field. Each morning, the team rented out the local Waffle House, and the players rolled in from their condos to the Waffle House for breakfast, and then to the stadium to play. On one particularly hot day, Bryan was in the midst of his normal routine when the White Sox personnel director came up to him, put a hand on his shoulder, and said "Bryan, it's time. You're going to the show."

Bryan almost had to pick his jaw up off the ground. The majors? Now?

"Get your stuff together, kid, you gotta go. The bus is waiting for you."

Bryan scrambled to get his catcher's gear packed into his bag and headed to the bus. He barely had time to catch his breath and process what was happening. The equipment managers threw his gear under the bus and Bryan climbed aboard. He quickly scanned the bus for a seat and his eyes came to rest on the last available seat, all the way in the back row. He then realized that sitting between him and that empty seat was an entire major league baseball team, made up of great ball players that he had looked up to for years. As he made his way to the back of the bus, he tried not to let the beads of sweat forming on his forehead give him away, but internally he was freaking out.

That day was one of the best days of Bryan's young adult life. The White Sox played the Red Sox, and he spent the day catching in the bullpen and reveling in the excitement of being a major league baseball player, if only for a day. That excitement was only made greater when Bryan heard his name shouted from the crowd, and turned to see a kid from his hometown waving at him.

And as soon as his day in the majors began, it was over. Bryan went back to the minor leagues, but after spring training that year, he got called up out of rookie ball and onto the Niagara Falls White Sox. After getting that call, he boarded a plane and flew to Niagara Falls, where he started to make a name for himself in the minor leagues, traveling around the northeast and really getting a taste for the professional baseball experience.

The Niagara Falls White Sox were scheduled to play the Chicago Cubs on their home turf at Sal Maglie Stadium. The two teams had something of a rivalry going on and had gotten into a little scuffle earlier in the season. The White Sox were on the field and Bryan was catching when the Cubs were up to bat. A young player not much older than Bryan stepped up to the plate. He was quick with his bat and had hit two home runs that night. Bryan threw a quick glance to his coach in the dugout, who told Bryan to signal to his pitcher to hit the batter. That didn't sit well with Bryan. He didn't like the idea of intentionally causing injury to another player, no matter how deep the rivalry.

Bryan threw the signal for a fastball inside. And when the pitch didn't hit the batter, his coach came storming out of the dugout and called a meeting on the mound, demanding to know why the batter wasn't hit.

"Hit him this time," the coach said through gritted teeth. And with the next pitch, the ball broke the batter's finger on his glove hand, ending his season.

A few innings later, Bryan came up to bat. Angry about their player who was hit, the Cubs retaliated. Their pitcher threw a ball straight for Bryan's head, and as he jerked backward to dodge it, he didn't pull back far enough and the ball went straight up under his helmet, hitting him in the left eye.

Bryan stumbled backward. His head was immediately spinning and it felt like he had been shot. Everything was hazy, and though muted, he could hear a collective "ooooh" exhaled from the crowd. It was hard for Bryan to figure out what was going on. It all happened so fast, but suddenly, he had a crowd around him and he was quickly realizing that he couldn't see out of his left eye.

"I'm blind. I'm going to be blind," he thought, a wave of panic washing over him.

The next few days were a blur. He was rushed to the hospital and then the team flew him to Chicago to meet with the White Sox team doctor and an eye specialist. After exam upon exam, Bryan heard the words he feared.

"Your retina is mangled. I can't reattach it. You're young, but there's nothing I can do for you," the doctor said.

Something about the way that he delivered the news said, "If I can't do something for you, no one can." He bandaged up Bryan's eye with gauze and a patch, and the next day Bryan was being wheeled through the airport in a wheelchair, his baseball career over. He couldn't help but think about how fast his life had changed. He had worked for years to play professional baseball and now here he was, just twenty years old, blind in his left eye and without any idea of what life would hold next.

Chapter 10

Out of Left Field

1985-2015

"For I know the plans I have for you," declares the Lord, "plans to prosper you and not to harm you, plans to give you hope and a future."
Jeremiah 29:11 (NIV)

When Bryan landed at the Philadelphia airport that day, he felt empty. His parents picked him up and as he sat in the backseat of their car on the ride to Reading, he couldn't help but wonder what was next. His vision in his left eye was totally gone, and the White Sox doctors hadn't left him with much hope of ever recovering it. His dream career was finished and his future was up in the air.

As his parents' car pulled up to the house that he grew up in, Bryan let out a sigh and opened the door. All he wanted to do was go to bed and wake up the next day and be back in the life he'd had just a few days earlier.

But life moves on, and so did Bryan. He made the decision to go back to school and pick up where he had left off. He went back to the place where he had first met Jesus, the Nazarene church, and started praying about what his next steps would be. As he started getting back into the familiar rhythm of life in Reading, Pennsylvania, he heard about the Mount Vernon Nazarene University in Ohio, and Bryan, ready for a new start, figured that was as good a place as any to get his degree. It would do him good to be surrounded by Christians, especially in a time when he felt so lost.

He started attending Mount Vernon as a business major that fall. His reputation preceded him and he was soon offered a job as an assistant coach for the school's baseball team. Bryan quickly became a popular figurehead in the athletic community. Other students were enamored with his career in the minor leagues, and his stories about his day facing the Red Sox while wearing a White Sox jersey alongside some of the greats only furthered his popularity.

Bryan hadn't been on campus long when he was invited to a meeting of the Fellowship of Christian Athletes. Hungry for community, he decided to go and check it out. He figured the least he could do would be to make a few friends and get to know some of his more athletically-inclined classmates. Somehow, in the course of that first meeting, he ended up being elected as the Vice President of the chapter. He also caught the eye of a certain girl in the club, Lynn Monday.

At the next meeting of the Fellowship of Christian Athletes, the club hosted a bonfire. Bryan was standing by the fire chatting with some friends when he spotted her across the crowd. Lynn's smile was infectious, and their eyes met for a brief second over the crackling flame of the fire. And in a second, a thought crossed Bryan's mind, "Hmm...I think I like Lynn."

Later that night, back in the apartment that he shared with five other guys, Bryan casually (and not so casually in the way that college-age guys do) asked about Lynn. His roommates saw right through the veil of cool that Bryan was trying to hide behind and one of them flew out of the apartment and down to where the girls' dorms were. He burst back into the apartment a few minutes later and exclaimed, "She's interested!" So Bryan decided that night that he would ask Lynn Monday out on a date.

A few days later, Lynn and Bryan met for their first date...to the library. Trying to keep things casual,

Bryan thought that the library would be a neutral, no pressure location. And also, he didn't really want Lynn to see his rust-mobile of a car. Lynn showed up ready to study with a book, but Bryan wasn't sure if he even owned a book. Instead, the pair sat and talked and just got to know one another over the course of the afternoon.

They soon started dating regularly, and it was quickly evident how good they were together. They were on fire for God and encouraged one another in their spiritual lives. And after about six months, Bryan borrowed a friend's car to take Lynn out on a real date. The two spent an evening traveling an hour away to Columbus, where they had dinner at Chi-Chi's, and while they laughed and talked, Bryan couldn't help but think that Lynn was one of the reasons God had brought him to Ohio.

Lynn eventually graduated from Mount Vernon and moved about two and a half hours away to Cincinnati while Bryan finished his business degree and the two continued their relationship long-distance. One day, he was sitting in chapel when he felt a familiar pang of conviction, the same thing that had come over him years earlier at the Nazarene church in Reading. The guest speaker that day asked everyone to close their eyes and imagine what their lives would look like if money didn't matter. What would they do? Where would they go?

All Bryan could think in that moment was, "I'd do something for Jesus."

He headed back to his room after the service had ended and he tried to shake the feeling that once again, something big had changed in his life. He laid in bed that night, trying to quiet his mind, but sleep wouldn't come. Around two o'clock in the morning, he couldn't take it anymore. He sat at his desk in his small apartment and started praying, and then he called his mom. He needed to talk to someone.

Donna answered the phone in a panic. Who could be calling in the middle of the night? As she listened to her son on the other end, tears started rolling down her cheeks. "Of course I'll pray, Bryan. Why don't you just spend the rest of the night praying and see what God has to say to you?" she asked her son before they hung up.

And that's exactly what Bryan did. He prayed until the sun rose, and in that time, he really felt God say, "If you let me, I'll use you."

Exhilarated and yet slightly confused, Bryan headed out across campus the next morning on the way to his first class, replaying what had happened the night before. Him? A pastor? Was God sure? He was so engrossed in his thoughts that he almost didn't see his sister, Marsha, who was also a student.

"Marsha! You're never going to believe this...I think I'm called to the ministry," Bryan could barely get the words out in his excitement.

Marsha was as stunned as Bryan felt the night before, "Have you talked to Lynn yet?"

Lynn. He had to call Lynn. They had been dating seriously for a while, and this had the power to change everything. After all, marrying someone in ministry wasn't for the faint of heart. She had to feel that calling too if their relationship could ever end in marriage.

A year earlier, Lynn had been sitting in her apartment at Mount Vernon, chatting with her girlfriends, when someone posed the question, "Would you want to marry a pastor?" The girls all agreed that that was the last thing they saw in their futures, and that marrying someone in ministry was the furthest thing from their future plans. Lynn agreed, but felt something unsettled in her spirit. That night, she prayed that she would be open to whatever God had in store for her life. When she answered the phone and heard about Bryan's calling, she couldn't help but chuckle. God certainly does have a sense of humor, doesn't he?

Bryan decided not to waste any time. He left school at Mount Vernon and enrolled in a new Bible college in Baton Rouge, Louisiana. Lynn already had a degree in physical education, but decided to follow Bryan to Baton Rouge, and enrolled in some elementary education classes, while also teaching gym at the Christian school on the campus. Since they weren't married, they lived on campus in the dorms.

It was the fall of 1986, and Bryan felt like he had finally found his calling and was on a path toward the future God had for him. When Valentine's day rolled around, Bryan was ready to take the next step toward his future. It was a sweltering hot February day in Louisiana, and Bryan asked Lynn out to dinner at the restaurant that started it all, Chi-Chi's. He nearly sweat right through the suit coat that he was wearing to conceal the small ring box in his pocket.

Lynn and Bryan got engaged on February 14, 1987, and after the spring semester finished, Bryan headed back to Reading to take a job and save money. The two wed on a gorgeous summer day on August 8, 1987, and then dove right back into Bible college just a few weeks later, this time as a married couple.

That spring, Bryan finished his degree and got licensed as a minister in the Assemblies of God. He had two years of a business degree and an associate's degree from Bible college, and a few years of professional baseball under his belt, but he had finally found his purpose. As they were nearing their first anniversary, Bryan and Lynn decided to move to Pottstown, Pennsylvania, just thirty minutes from Bryan's parents. Lynn took a job at a local Assemblies of God college, and Bryan started putting out his resumes while he continued working at the same place he had the summer before just to keep them afloat.

Every resume was met with silence. Churches of six people wouldn't even interview him. But one young pastor named Tom caught Bryan's resume and put it in front of Pastor James Swank, who was leading a growing church in the Reading area. Pastor Swank decided to give Bryan a chance and offered him an internship at GT Church that paid $50 per week. And that December, Pastor Swank called Bryan into his office and offered him a job.

Taking the job at GT meant taking a 75% pay cut from the job he was working to support his family. When Bryan called his boss, he was offered a company car to stay. He turned down that offer, telling his boss that he was called into ministry. "Well, if that church thing doesn't work out, you'll always have a job with us," his boss said before hanging up with Bryan.

Bryan stepped out in faith and never looked back. He was on staff at GT for four years when he and Lynn decided that they were going to buy a house. They found a small row home in Reading that they could afford on his modest pastor's salary, and they were excited to make their first home purchase together.

One day in the fall of 1991, Pastor Swank and Bryan were headed to a meeting together. Bryan was sitting in the passenger seat of Pastor Swank's car, when he excitedly delivered the news. "We're going to buy a house!"

"You're going to buy a house?" Pastor Swank stammered.

"Yeah! We're going to buy a house!" Bryan said again.

"No, you're not," Pastor Swank said, his words heavy. Bryan looked at him, bewildered.

"Bryan, I wasn't going to tell you this, but I need you to know something," Pastor Swank started, choosing his words carefully. "I'm going to retire. And when I do, the bylaws of GT state that you'll need to tender your resignation too. So you can't buy a house. And you can't tell anyone."

Bryan sat, stunned. He and Lynn were on the cusp of an exciting new step in their lives. Their first son,

Ben, had just turned one in June. They were building careers and a family and making plans for their future, and now all of it might come crashing to a halt. He and Lynn took Pastor Swank's advice and didn't buy the house that they had picked out. And in January of 1992, Pastor Swank announced his retirement and recommended that the board make Bryan the new Senior Pastor of GT.

On a brisk night in February, Bryan and Lynn sat nervously in the house next to the church as the congregation voted on their fate. They didn't have to wait long before the verdict came in. Bryan won 99-1, and in that moment, life really changed.

The Sunday after Easter, Bryan preached his first message as the senior pastor. Bryan and Lynn moved into the house next to the church and in 1993, welcomed their second son, Bryce, into their growing family. GT was growing as well and soon it was evident that they needed to pray about making a big move.

There was a large parcel of land a few minutes away that was up for sale. In total, it was about eight acres and was going for around $70,000 per acre. Bryan felt God saying that this was going to be the future of GT, but that was hard to imagine with a church that had $117 in its building fund. They launched a building campaign called "Building for the Harvest," and the owners of the land decided to give the church a discount because they thought "a nice little quiet church would be nice." Little did they know that little and quiet weren't really words that were in God's plans for GT. The church moved to the new location in 1997, and that same year Lynn and Bryan welcomed their third son, Brett, into their family.

The couple was thriving. They were pastoring a church that was on fire for God and raising three God-honoring kids. And as their family grew, Bryan and Lynn found new hobbies that they loved to do together. They both discovered that they found great joy in riding motorcycles. They loved spending time together on an open road on the back of a bike, and took rides every once in a while on Ted's old bike. In 2009, they bought their first Harley Davidson and entered a whole new phase of their love for motorcycles. Donna hated that they rode bikes, but Lynn loved doing it.

One day, when Donna was expressing her concern for their safety, Lynn said, "Donna, if I die on the back of a Harley Davidson, I'll die a happy person." Donna never bothered them about it again, but she prayed fervently for them any time they headed out on a ride.

By 2015 GT was entering a new season of growth, and so were Bryan and Lynn. Lynn was getting ordained by the Assemblies of God in May and their family was growing with the arrival of their first grandchild later that year.

Bryan had just gotten home from a trip to Africa and was sitting in his office one day in the spring of 2015 when he got a phone call. He picked up the phone and was surprised to find Ruth Jarvis on the other end of the line. Ruth's daughter, Liz, was the girl that had led Bryan to Jesus all those years earlier when he was in high school. Ruth and her husband were getting ready to move out of the state, but were so amazed at what God was doing through Bryan and GT that they had a bit of a unique donation they wanted to make to the church before they moved.

As it turns out, the couple had purchased two gravesites, caskets, and other funeral arrangements for themselves before they had made the decision to move. Now that they were going to retire in another state to be closer to their children, they had no use for the burial plots or other arrangements, and thought that perhaps the church could hold onto them to give to a family who might need them someday.

Bryan consulted with some of the pastors on staff, who were hesitant to take such a unique donation, but something in Bryan's spirit said to just take them; maybe there would be a family they could help someday. Little did he know, it would be his own family who was in need of one of those plots just a few months later.

May 6, 2015: Lynn was ordained at GT Church one month before the accident. (Pictured left to right: Ronda, Bryan, Lynn, Renee.)
Photo courtesy of Brenda Bohner.

Chapter 11

Left Leg

October-December, 2015

A shoot will come up from the stump of Jesse; from his roots a Branch will bear fruit.
Isaiah 11:1 (NIV)

By mid-October, a lot was changing in Bryan's life. He was reaching new milestones in his recovery and moving forward toward getting his first prosthetic leg, and he was reaching milestones in his personal life as well when he became a grandfather at the birth of his grandson, Jackson. Some of these milestones were exciting because they meant progress, and others were bittersweet as they made him miss Lynn even more than he already did.

After his return on Sunday, October 18, Bryan was back. He had such a great return to GT and was ready to dive back into ministry full-time. The next Sunday he traveled to GT's multi-site campus to greet the church there, and throughout the week he was back in meetings and moved into his newly-renovated office.

The next month seemed to fly by as he got back into the swing of things. It was good to be back to work; at church, he felt like himself again. He was normal, and being there was a strong, safe, healing place for him.

Bryan worked on catching up on everything he had missed in between therapy and prosthesis appointments. He went through the process of being molded for a leg, and even got to help design what the socket that would go over his thigh would look like.

Before anyone knew it, Thanksgiving was on the horizon. Each year, GT holds a Thanksgiving Eve service called Around the Table. It's a family service, meant to bring everyone together just to celebrate Thanksgiving as a church family. Bryan was planning to be there and to spend time in fellowship with the church, but that morning he had to have his nineteenth surgery.

One of the first procedures that had been done to him following the accident on June 7 was to implant an umbrella-like filter into a major vein, designed to catch and stop any potential blood clots from reaching his heart. When Ben had signed the form authorizing the doctors to implant the device nearly six months earlier, it had been a hard decision. The implanting surgery was not without risks, the most threatening of which was that the device could potentially dislodge and end up killing Bryan. Ben hadn't taken the initial decision lightly, but had ultimately decided, under the advice of Bryan's doctors, that the benefits outweighed the risks.

Early on the morning of Wednesday, November 25, 2015, Ted took Bryan to the hospital for what they hoped would be his final surgery. Bryan was nervous, and the process of removing the filter seemed just as complicated and risk-filled as the process of putting it in. After going through all of the paperwork, he was ready. Ted prayed with him before the surgical team got him prepped for surgery.

Because of the high-risk nature of the surgery, the team opted to keep Bryan awake throughout the procedure. Not putting him under general anesthesia meant a lower risk of a number of serious side effects.

"You might feel some discomfort," an anesthesiology nurse warned him, "but we're ready to put you out at any point if the need arises."

It was a life-changing experience for Bryan. He laid there, trying to stay perfectly still as the surgeon opened his jugular vein and inserted a cable down the vein. And as he watched the cable go down his vein on a TV screen, he couldn't help but think, "I can't believe this is my life." The whole procedure only took twenty minutes, and it seemed that just as soon as the cable went down his vein, it was coming back up with the filter in tow. And just like that, it was over.

The surgeon patched Bryan up and sent him on his way, and that night Bryan went to church under strict orders not to lift anything over ten pounds and to take it easy.

The service that night was the perfect mix of light-heartedness and depth. It felt like a gathering of family, and Bryan loved being with his church family that night, but in the back of his mind, he knew the next day was going to be hard.

He spent Thanksgiving at his mom and dad's house, the table full of his mom's cooking, topped off with her famous homemade cheesecake. It was great to gather with his family, but the day had a heaviness to it. It was the first major holiday that they were spending without Lynn, and though they were gathered around the table together, they all knew that there was an empty seat.

The Koch Thanksgiving tradition included each person having a Scripture verse on his or her plate.

Before dinner, they'd go around the circle and each read their Scripture and then say one thing that they were grateful for. When it came to Bryan, his list was nearly a mile long. He could have talked all afternoon, but mostly that year, he was grateful for life. As they worked their way from each person to the next, the emotion in the room was bittersweet. They were all happy to have Bryan sitting there, but all felt the loss of Lynn in a deep way that day.

For Bryan, facing the holidays without his wife was difficult. Every event, every family tradition, every new milestone for his grandson was simultaneously a joyous moment and a reminder that she wasn't there to witness any of it. Bryan was struggling with trying to figure out who he was. He was different, he knew that, but he was working to rediscover the old Bryan Koch as he began adjusting to his new normal.

In an effort to keep things positive, the family decided that they'd honor all of the Koch holiday traditions, from picking out and cutting down the Christmas tree to the annual get together at Ronda's house, where Bryan filled his usual spot at the stove making each person their personalized order of eggs.

As the Christmas season took hold, Bryan got the news that his leg was ready. He had passed his home therapy and it was determined that his hips had healed enough to be able to start walking again. In early December he headed back to the Reading Hospital's in-patient rehab to learn the intricacies of walking with a prosthetic leg.

Bryan's leg was waiting for him at the rehab, and it amazed him how much effort it took to put it on. It seemed to take hours. He quickly fell into the routine of rehab. Each day he'd get up, shower, eat breakfast, and then start the ever-arduous task of putting on his leg. First, he'd layer on socks to protect his residual leg as he inserted it into the socket of the prosthesis. Then, he'd strap on the prosthetic leg and with help from the nursing staff, he'd head to his first therapy session of the day.

The leg itself cost over $50,000 and was state of the art. So state of the art, in fact, that most therapists were still learning about it. His particular leg was designed with a beginner in mind. It was sluggish and wasn't designed to optimize its highest potential, but it was exactly what Bryan needed as he learned how to put one foot in front of the other again.

At first, he could barely even get his leg to bend. Bryan marveled at just how much there was to think about when walking. Most people never have to think about it, but walking is a complicated process.

Heel strikes, hip flexes, gait, flexibility, balance. It was a lot to keep in mind and it was all exhausting. His therapist, Karen, would take videos of him during therapy for him to review so that he could see just how his leg was bending and moving.

After his morning therapy, Bryan would head back to his room, rest, eat lunch, take medicine, and gear up for an afternoon of more therapy. At night, he'd lay awake, trying to get his mind to rest, thinking about his family and GT and going over his therapy sessions in his head. With time, it became easier and he learned how to move his leg more naturally.

On December 17, in the middle of his rehab stay, Bryan took a day off to head to the Berks County Courthouse. It was the day of the hearing for the man who had hit him and Lynn, and he was going to testify and confess to all that he had done that day.

Due to the media coverage surrounding Bryan's case, the court had arranged for his case to be heard last on what they deemed "DUI Thursday," a day full of hearings for people charged with driving under the influence. As Bryan sat waiting, surrounded by his family members, he breathed a deep sigh. A lady in the waiting room was telling stories of other DUI hearings, about people with stories that mirrored Bryan's and Lynn's. Finally, Bryan heard his case called.

The courtroom was tiny and filled quickly with members of Bryan's family and people from GT. Bryan was seated at a table, and inches away from him sat the family of the driver, the weight that they had been bearing for months evident. This story was not just one that the Koch family had been living, but one that was much more far-reaching. They had an opportunity to speak on behalf of the defendant, and they told the court about how he was a good person, how he helped others, and how important he was to his wife and young children. His wife sat behind a table, tears rolling down her cheeks.

Ronda and Renee had prepared letters to the man who had killed their sister, and there wasn't a dry eye in the room as they read their emotional accounts of how the events of June 7 had changed their lives forever. Ben spoke briefly and then Bryan took the floor. He addressed the man who killed his wife directly that day...

"Choices matter. We make our choices and they make us, and you chose to do what you did on June 7th and it caused my family a lot of hurt. But you have a choice today. Today, you can choose to help your family and to choose God's forgiveness."

Bryan's words were short and full of grace. He had already forgiven the man who was sitting in front of him, and what had happened couldn't be undone. But now, what Bryan really wanted was for this man and his family to find Jesus. Because without Him, true change couldn't happen in their lives. The judge sentenced him to prison, effective that day, and he was led away to be taken to the Berks County prison. And with that, the legal chapter of the story was closed.

The man's aunt approached Bryan in the courtroom after the hearing. She had been to GT multiple times, and as she walked up to Bryan words escaped her. All she could say was how sorry she was and how much she wanted her nephew to find Christ.

Once the court proceedings were over, Bryan headed back to rehab and just like that, jumped back into therapy and learning to use his new leg.

A few days later, Bryan left rehab once again, this time with his therapist, and headed to GT for a walk-through of the Christmas Eve services. GT's six services were planned for December 23 and 24 and Bryan would be preaching at each one of them. He and his therapist met some of the GT staff and spent an hour walking around the church and practicing how he would move on stage. When he left, he was confident that he was ready to walk out onto the GT stage for the first time since June 7. Bryan and his therapist finished the afternoon with an occupational therapy session in the way of grocery shopping, and then they headed back to the rehab hospital for Bryan's last few days.

On Christmas Eve, the services opened with worship and some announcements, and then the room went dark. A video started playing detailing some of the items on Bryan's 2014 Christmas wish list...a Starbucks card, a White Sox jersey, a Harley Davidson jacket. And then, the list was replaced by Bryan's 2015 list, which only had one item: a new leg. The crowd exploded when that item was checked off and their pastor walked out onto the stage, free of the wheelchair and walker they had grown accustomed to seeing him with over the prior two months.

Bryan took a moment to soak in all of the emotion he was sharing with the congregation and, taking a deep breath, began to speak. His message that evening focused on stumps. There were tree stumps lining the stage, illuminated by the soft glow of candlelight, and a stump where Bryan sat, holding a crown of thorns. He talked about the stumps in our lives and the stump of Jesse, and he talked about how life isn't defined by what is removed, and how even out of the stumps in life, God can grow new things.

At the end of his message was GT's traditional Christmas Eve candle lighting. Bryan took center stage, holding his candle as Jen, holding Jackson, joined him from backstage. The worship center was aglow with thousands of small flickering flames. As they stood there, taking in the magnificence of the moment, *O Holy Night* swelling behind them, neither one of them could stop the hot tears from falling down their cheeks. The sight in front of them was beautiful, and there was so much beauty in the fact that Bryan was alive to see it.

Afterward

Left Assured

Maybe you feel like you've been left holding the bag because of life's circumstances. But I want to assure you that you can be "all right."

In the first message that I preached after the accident, I shared the story of Moses leading the Israelites out of Egypt. Here they were, the entire nation of Israel, at the foot of the Red Sea with the Egyptian army close behind. Between a rock and a hard place. And what does God do? He parts the sea, and they walk right through.

Fast forward a bit and you'll find those same Israelites wandering around in the hot, dry desert, complaining that God hasn't delivered them into the Promised Land, and forgetting God's past provision. The problem is, they were living in the future instead of seeking God in their present. They couldn't be patient and wait for God's plan to unfold, and like the psalmist says in Psalm 106:13-14, *"But they soon forgot what he had done and did not wait for his plan to unfold. In the desert they gave in to their craving; in the wilderness they put God to the test." (NIV)*

The Israelites learned the power of forgetting and the problem with sameness. When you're in a difficult season, it's all too easy to focus on your circumstances and what's happening right now. Trust me, I know! 2015 was undoubtedly one of the hardest years I've ever been through. Facing the birth of our first grandson without Lynn, and then going through the holidays without her was painful. And it could have been easy to wonder where God was in all of this.

But there's importance in remembering, when you're walking in the deepest of valleys, the things that God has done in your past. And there's hope and joy in seeking out the ways God is working in your present pain. If biblical hope is confident expectation and biblical joy is intentional and eternal, then being hopeful and joyful in hard circumstances is a choice.

We wake up each day and have to make the choice to find hope and joy in the ways God is working in the present, because whether we can see it or not, He has already made a way through it.

There's a Swahili proverb that uses the phrase "haba na haba," which translates to "little by little" and has become something of a motto for me. In times of blinding pain and grief, in times of great difficulty, when we reach those hard places, God brings us through. We might not see the big picture and we might not know the path, but little by little, He guides us.

If God brings you to it, He'll bring you through it. All we need to do is remember what God did in our past, look for God in our present, and trust God with our future.

I've lost my left eye, my left leg, and the wedding ring off my left finger, but because of God's grace, mercy, and incredible love, *I'm All Right.*

I am trusting that wherever life's circumstances have left you, you will find hope, strength, and joy knowing that God is right beside you with every step you take.

Strong and Surrendered,
Bryan Koch

For additional resources, visit:
bryankoch.org
gtaog.org
learningtofollow.net

Acknowledgments

Bryan would like to thank the following people for their help in sharing his story:

Ben and Jen Koch
Bryce and Sarah Koch
Brett Koch
Ted and Donna Koch
Marsha Koch
Renee Neiswender
Ronda Neiswender
Betsy Fick
Staci Focht
Lisa Nuss
Deb Bube

Above all else, Bryan would like to acknowledge the strength and grace of God that have brought him through this experience.

BRYAN KOCH is the Lead Pastor at GT Church in Reading, PA, where he has served for over 25 years. Drawing on his incredible life experiences, Bryan communicates with an authentic, open style that allows him to be transparent and real with people. Most of all, he is able to share about his unwavering faith that has taught him that if God brings you to it, he will bring you through it. In addition to leading a church of over 3,000, Bryan is the co-author of the discipleship book Follow, and is also a frequent conference speaker, specializing in coaching churches in leadership development. However, Bryan's true passion is helping people become fully devoted followers of Jesus.

BETSY FICK is a writer and photographer based in southeastern Pennsylvania who loves inspiring others towards a closer walk with Jesus through her writing. Betsy and her husband, AJ, live in Leesport, PA with their pup, Quincy. They both work in ministry at GT Church and are lucky to be able to pursue various creative passions side by side.